THE GATHERING

This is my story,
the words on this page
aren't just words?
They are from the
sounds of my soul.

My frustrations and
angers follow me daily.
I thought that if
I put this on paper
I might be able to confront
them with your help.

anonymous

The Gathering

CITY PRAYERS,
CITY HOPES

COMPILED AND EDITED BY

Jeannine Otis

SEABURY BOOKS
IS AN IMPRINT OF
CHURCH PUBLISHING INCORPORATED, NEW YORK

The gathering : city prayers, city hopes / compiled and edited by Jeannine Otis.
    p. cm.
  ISBN 978-1-59627-045-9 (pbk.)
  1. Prayers. I. Otis, Jeannine.

BV245.G38 2007
242—dc22
        2007004883

Church Publishing, Incorporated.
445 Fifth Avenue
New York, New York 10016

5   4   3   2   1

Contents

Part 3: Our Light

Part 4: We Are Powerful Beyond Measure

Part 5: Your Voice

Foreword

Worship the Lord in the beauty of Holiness
—Psalm 96.9

Hip Hop is rich, it is beautiful, it is of God. Walking with Jeannine Otis in my South Bronx neighborhood several years ago, when we first met, I pointed up toward the two dozen or more "PJ" high-rises (as our children and young people call their homes) and stated, "This is our church... These are the 'Cathedral' pillars... The children and young people are not merely our 'future' but our 'today'!" She, like me, was inspired that day beholding the beauty and holiness with which God surrounds us at every turn. So does God *gather*! How can we not gather?

Jeannine Otis's insightfulness and love bring us to *The Gathering*.

We can celebrate beauty in shiny "bling" cross and in jewel-studded processional cross, great old Victorian Gothic and in bare Pentecostal storefront, in classical prelude and in rhythmic loop, rap, and dance, in great numbers and small. Beauty – God – abounds if we will but approach and embrace those "connecting points of life," as Jeannine calls them, at Street or Altar, troubling or joyful, risky or "good bet."

We are *gathered* by the Love of God in All and for All – in the humanity that God gives to Everybody, Everywhere. This is the beauty – the holiness – to which God calls us: *To love God and to love our neighbors as ourselves*! And this is a little corner of its story – *The Gathering*.

I remember that day, walking with Jeannine, the love and beauty she affirmed in my neighborhood, in me – and in the people – the hospitality and love she evoked with each passing child and mother, old man and young. Beauty was reflected in one another. *Is this not God?* This was the first of countless neighborhood walks and Altar Celebrations she would lead. She helped me to know and celebrate the great beauty – hip hop and not – of the "gathering" on the streets of the "South, South Bronx" that day and on many days and nights to come.

As a founder of HipHopEMass she has helped hundreds – thousands – of others celebrate this great beauty. *Is this not Love?* In this wonderful text, Jeannine and the poets, people of prayer, and writers she has gathered help all of us appreciate a little more deeply the beauty of holiness – the expressions and desires of the hearts of the People of God. Gathered here are beautiful prayers of classic tradition and newer hip hop tradition representing global community, faith new and old! God's Love is boundless and without end.

A reporter recently asked while holding forth a copy of *The Hip Hop Prayer Book* (from the creation of which *The Gathering* was born), "Is this yours?" I was a little confused for a moment not knowing what was being asked. "*Is this yours?*" I asked back. "Does it belong to Kanye West or Nas or...?" pressed the interviewer. "No, no, no..." I replied. "This book is original – from our children and young people!" The surprise in his face made my heart sing! The same is true here, and already my heart sings!

And you know what? In cities and towns across America and the world, the wealth and beauty, the yearnings and hopes of many more children and young people wait to be heard and celebrated – to be gathered and beloved as here in *The Gathering*. The love, the beauty, the abundance of God overwhelm!

Thank you and bless you Jeannine, contributors and writers for *The Gathering*.

God celebrates and loves each of you as you shout out your love to a God. Our God does not stop, will not stop. Love is Her Word for ever and ever!

Thank You, God, for Gathering All Your People!

ONE!

Poppa T + NYC
Timothy Holder (The Revd.)
Founding Priest and Pastor
HipHopEMass
698 East 166th Street
Bronx, New York 10456
www.HipHopEMass.org

Introduction

A New Pentecost
by Canon Lloyd S. Casson

When that day had come, they were all together in the one place. Now there were people from every hue and tribe, young children, older youth and adults of all ages, and they spoke many "languages." Some spoke the language of the rich, some of the poor, some spoke in the tongue of those living in the mainstream of society and others of those living on the edge, some spoke with happy words, and some with hurting ones, some spoke the languages of the confident and fulfilled, some spoke the language of the knowledge of God, some spoke in a cursing language—to God and to everyone and to everything; and some barely spoke at all.

And suddenly, from all around came the powerful sounds of drums, music and the rhythmic cadences of hip hop, in prayer and praise and testimony. And all of them were filled with the Holy Spirit, and in their own "languages" they heard the Good News of Jesus Christ.

In *The Gathering*, Jeannine Otis, like a Pied Piper, summons all who will come, to a celebration of the Good News in Christ in a Hip Hop Mass, and where the Children and the Elders teach and learn from each other about the transforming implications of that Good News for their own lives and the life of the world.

It was my great pleasure to work directly with Jeannine as a colleague at St. Mark's Church in-the-Bowery, where she continues to be the Director of Music. A profoundly spiritual person, she is also a consummate church musician who loves and respects the liturgical forms of the Church. With great skill and sensitivity she introduces, blends, and weaves throughout the liturgy—incorporating the world's church, classical, popular and contemporary—into the regular Sunday and other worship services and events. The results are phenomenal for making those services relevant to the lives of all who are participating. Everyone present experiences God of the Ages acknowledging their own personal pain and aspirations.

As far as hip hop goes, Jeannine has been working in that culture for many years, and as a special arts teacher in many of New York's public schools, she is fluent in the language of hip hop culture. She holds workshops for the students, bringing them in direct touch with successful hip hop and other artists, and teaches them (frees them) to rap in spoken word and in song, their deepest concerns, longings, faith, hope, and their own prayers. Given this scenario, hip hop masses and other such events at St. Mark's were just a matter of time for Jeannine.

The genius of *The Gathering* is that in it, members of the hip hop culture and of other cultures are released from their respective boxes. People all across the spectrum—youth, young adult, middle aged, and elders, and of whatever culture or "language" or hue—are enabled to see themselves, and to see Christ in one another. Thus, the dividing walls of suspicion, fear, and prejudice are broken down, and the Kingdom of God becomes a reality.

Give the growing pervasiveness of the hip hop "genre" in our culture in general—especially among children, teens and young adults—*The Gathering*, in my estimation, has the potential for being a dynamic instrument for Christian evangelism.

Hip Hop in the Church?

It's wonderful. Embrace it. God's love don't stop. Amen. Word!

Peace,
Canon Lloyd S. Casson

Why We Gather

When I was a child my mother was deeply involved in the fight for human rights, through that Dr. King made a special effort to meet with her and, by extension, me. A long time after, I realized that I was affected just by being around these people who saw the power of the connections that all people have between one another. It was a lesson that's taken years to sink in and to learn. I'm still learning it.

The purpose of this book is to celebrate life and that connection. It is to remember that we are all one. It is too easy to forget our ultimate connection as human beings when so much of what we encounter in everyday life promotes separation.

One of the most profound revelations I've had in my life is the feeling of being connected to all that is. That feeling is the joy that has propelled my spirit to want to continue and find the truth in everything I do. We are never alone. We are God's people. We come in a beautiful array of varieties and our natural spiritual state is one of beauty.

All journeys toward truth and the good news are full of unexpected twists and turns. My own continues to be full of those twists and turns and on many occasions they have led me to some places where there was no hope. I have battled depression, physical illness, family discord, the loss of those who seemed to make life bearable, and betrayal. There were times when I just wanted to end the whole life dance. I even tried. Even in the worst of those times there always seemed to be something to be connected to. A person or a song that would pick me up, cliché as it sounds.

Connecting and reconnecting with friends, many of whom are my colleagues in the music business (and many of whom have contributed to this book), reconnecting with family—understanding and forgiving—and giving and receiving unconditional love that is real is not easy. When I speak of overcoming that's what I'm referring to. I'm still a work in progress, we all are, but I'm much closer now because of the connections and unconditional love that I have experienced. Because of gathering. Just the other day I woke up and said:

Thank you God and the Universe for all that is. We continue to find connections that propel us into the light...

Jeannine Otis

PART 1

Our Deepest Fear

911

Clock arms passing eight, then nine
Devil arms reaching out to tear a perfect day
Human arms flapping, pouring out of windows like wine,

Thousands and thousands and thousands of voices,

Shrieking O God, O God.

Kareem Davis

Keep Your Head Up

Overcast future and the past riding on a dime
no control ever will keep hold of my life
but inside the darkest night is the day
So I listen to the words of life that I heard my father say

He said:
Keep your head up to the sky don't be shy
Trust in what you know is right and I'll provide

Can't find a job for money will rob or do I have to sling
(don't mean a thing)
Question fate who do I have to hate in order to be great?
But if love is the key what else do I need to be a success?
(I wanna be blessed)
Believing in the one is how I've begun to be great

Keep your head up to the sky don't be shy
Trust in what you know is right and I'll provide

You know in life we go through so much
We'll all get there if we don't give up
Live Life like you won't know tomorrow
And you might lose all of your pain and sorrow

Keep your head up to the sky don't be shy
Trust in what you know is right and I'll provide

Edwin Lugo

Untitled

Father I pray for your wisdom and courage
As these prison bars play a cat and mouse game with my mind
I pray that you will remove the shadows of loneliness
    from my life
and bless my days though........ they seem
numbered...........according to your will.

Incarcerated Youth, USA

Untitled

I feel caged in this place
The pain is overwhelming
THERE HAS TO BE A DIFFERENT WAY
I hurt so much HELP
Help me today
I put my trust in you Lord Jesus

Incarcerated Youth, USA

Inside Boo

The way I feel,
I feel like a dime.
When I don't, I feel like nobody
I feel like I'm not there, or I feel
out of control.

I feel like I want to talk.
No one listens.
I just wanted someone to listen
when I talk, I cry sometimes.

But sometimes I stay strong.

Betty Diaz

Stresss

Stress. Stress. Stress. Not the best. I can't get by without the smoke of a cigarette. I'm trapped and caged, held down with chains, thrown in a cell like a slave. I'm a minority in the Divided States of America. People always treating me like I'm a nigga, but I get past that. I'm filled with anger. And I'm confused. I'm put to work like a slave. And I'm being used. Man. I'm so depressed. Stress. Stress. Stress.

Joel Encarnacion

Hustle Hard

Money hurts
Kill for it, steal for it, die for it,
do anything for it.

Do it for better
not for worse.

We do it cause we have to
not cause we want to.
Hustle hard, hustle sweat

Remember man, protect your heart.

Marcus Rivers

When I am Mad

When I am mad and out of control,
I just don't know.
How to go to a place where
I can take it slow.

People make me mad
when they don't leave me alone.

Talking about
my business,
my family,
and my home.

Make me lose control,
makes me want to fight.

Body heats up
muscles get tight
words start flying
like windy kites.
Tail start whipping
punching, hitting, kicking.
Try to hold me back.

John Anthony

Faith

Children crying, people dying in the streets
Patrolling, protecting, parading
Black tides/white reefs—
Take care!! Take care!!
I am a cop

Kareem Davis

Untitled

Lord WHO AM I??????
Other people call me many names that walk with me
    in this physical form
But WHO AM I TO YOU
AM I a gift or a curse??????
My heart wants me to maintain a positive attitude
But some people make it hard...make it ugly
why are these people at my party.........I have inherited
    what they are
they are blocking my soul's peace
I am a kind caring person, but why are these people
    around me????
What are you trying to tell me?????
Am I an ugly person inside????
What are you trying to tell me????
WHO AM I??????????
AM I a gift or a curse??????
WHO AM I????
WHO AM I?????

Incarcerated Youth, USA

PART 2:

Our Darkness

Road Trip

From foster to Harlem
Outside the building

Discovering everything I don't
Need to know

Jonathan Reyes

Untitled

This is my story,
the words on this page
aren't just words?
They are from the
sounds of my soul.

My frustrations and
angers follow me daily.
I thought that if
I put this on paper
I might be able to confront
them with your help.

anonymous

Untitled

Lord, What is my purpose ?
Why am I a victim of circumstance?
Am I on the right track?
I am left in the tunnel with no light, no sense of direction
Though my faith is strong I'm tired of my present position
I pray daily for your mercy and favor
I'm going to continue to humble myself to your will and
    your way of life
Protect and guide me thru this storm so at the end there I will
    see the light
Be my Lighthouse and bring me home
AMEN

Incarcerated Youth, USA

Storm Warning

Children of the storm
Forced out, thrust out,
Expelled from the womb.

Standing knee-deep in water, dying of thirst.

Abandoned deserted,
Straddling the tomb.

Reaching out of life, yet fearing the worst.

Joshua Reyes

Untitled

A poor soul it is, borne to a fake melting pot,
nothing but division, unity had been shot,
the boy is a creature, a dweller of the street,
probed or pleasured by all those he meets.
I wanna leave this place I think, my pen scrapes across
    the paper,
I wanna leave now but I must wait till later.

I'm on a train to hell and there's no getting off.
I'm pulling the emergency break but the train won't stop.
Bam Bam Bam goes the hammer on the train line,
I am I am I am goes the hammer in my mind.

I woke to a gray, stagnant sorry day,
yet I keep on breathing – I know no other way.
What a glory it must be, to be a stranger of the street,
to not have met the danger I've had too meet.
I wonder how I might be
I wonder now how my eyes would see.

I'm on a train to hell and there's no getting off.
I'm pulling the emergency break but the train won't stop.
Bam Bam Bam goes the hammer on the train line,
I am I am I am goes the hammer in my mind.

My bullets as my ballots, now I cast my final vote.
With a pull of the trigger I shoot my oppressor through
    the throat.
I shoot down ignorance, shattering fear.

I couldn't kill hatred, but I was pretty damn near.
There're six vast armies clashing in my mind.
Who will be the victor I'll have to learn in time.

I'm on a train to hell and there's no getting off.
I'm pulling the emergency break but the train won't stop.
Bam Bam Bam goes the hammer on the train line,
I am I am I am goes the hammer in my mind.

Jacob Sharerz Schoenbaum

Untitled

Dear Lord Jesus we bow down to you
Time could be hard and you help us get through

He's got my back and that's why I breathe

On the bad times he's made evil cease
We Black, Spanish, White and we pray to you
at night
Don't wanna do us wrong
He wants to lead us right

Mariah Morris

Utterances

Either I walk my journey or I'll be dragged along—this is a
truth that would not be lost again. I did not want to be a writer
and usually found myself a broken seeker. The belated rain of
winter lore reminded me that I had

wandered from His will. Not writing became like living later
and there was no language for wounds or a kiss or a memory
tumbling forth. I fell far from my source and life passed as
though it were simple, but with so

much road to travel still, I know I must write. I have to because
I will die otherwise. I pray that my guts catch up to my mission
in life and hold onto the whisper just beyond the page: My life-
work is who I am

I surrender to my purpose and write what moves in soul. The
rest, I leave in God's hands.

Michelle Heath

God Make Me Your Mirror

God make me your mirror
*Through practice, we become not just the image of, but the mirror
for, God*
—Gregory of Nyssa

God who made me in your image
I would be your mirror
God make me your mirror

make my surface clean and smooth,
    wash me clear of the grime of envy,
      the smudge of resentment, the fingerprint of lust.
cleanse me with the soap of stillness, the spray of silence,
    buff me with the linen of holy reading
      and wipe me bright with psalms.
Make my surface smooth and clean,

    make me your mirror, God

make my edges true and strong—
    free me from the warp of vanity
    from the bulge of distraction
balance me with the level of faith,
    set me in a frame of love,
    fix me on the walls of the House of the LORD
make my edges strong and true.

make me your mirror, God

make my center pure
    drive far from my heart the fear
        of sin
        of the devils
        of death
    take my shattered heart and make it whole

God you made me in your image
I will be your mirror
God make me your mirror

anonymous

I Have a Dream Too

I have a Dream
that niggas will get along

I have a Dream
that niggas will stop calling each other niggas.

I have a Dream
one day niggas will stop fighting each other.

I have a Dream
that White people will stop calling "nigga" to each other.

I have a Dream
that music
—rap and hip hop—
will stop putting "nigga" in songs.

Michael Barreto

Untitled

Pulling us apart and intervening
next thing I know I with the dean.
     Stories get told
     decisions get made
     for now it's over.
Tomorrow it's a new day.
Control is the word.
Positive is the way.
Ignoring is helpful
don't bother what they say.

anonymous

PART 3:

Our Light

Hip-Hopper's Prayer

Almighty God, help me to be
the Christian person that You see
not the boy inside of me
with fears and insecurity
or what my elders constantly
say lacks signs of civility.

Comfort me, dear God above
with Your true eternal love.
Help me know that You are near
to keep me safe and free from fear.

Almighty God, set my eyes
on Your love full of surprise
so that I'm not hypnotized
by guys who tend to glamorize
their macho claims and cunning lies
and language elders criticize.

God, walk beside each boy and girl
within whom you have placed a pearl
of wisdom and abiding grace.
It's Your love that we should embrace.

Neil Braxton Gibson

The Reason Why I Sing

I love to be happy
to be happy that is the reason why I sing
Just to feel the peace and joy it brings
That is the reason why I sing
And when I'm feeling shy and scared, and think of
    my great song
All my shyness and fears are swept away, and my sadness gone.
God makes me sing
Just to put happiness and love in me.
God loves me with all his heart and soul
That's the reason that I sing

At times I may be shy.
But when I sing to God he grants to me
the strength to breathe and carry on.
Someone may be asking
why am I so shy.
What I'm trying to say through these few words
is that I am just a private guy.

But most importantly, I must be sure you all know this
when I lift my head up high and sing,
God helps me to fly up unto him,
the reason why I sing.

anonymous

Untitled

It's comforting to know that when it was proclaimed that
    I was made in Your image.
That it's the soul, and not the body that was meant.
It's comforting to know that when I talk to myself I'm talking
    to You,
when I talk to someone else that I'm talking to You.
It's comforting to know that because of this I am never
    without You.
Therefore,
I am never alone as I wander through this wonderment
    called Life
wrapped in the comfort of Your Love.

Larry Marshall

Untitled

Thank you for this day, dear Lord. Be with me in it to guide and strengthen me. As the unfolding hours present me with choices both great and small, help me choose what you would have me choose, those thoughts, words and actions which build up instead of destroy, encourage instead of demean, help rather than harm. Help me remember you presence within me, even as I recognize your presence in others so that I may treat everyone, including myself, with respect. If the going gets rough, let me join my suffering to yours on the cross, so that I may hope with you in God's power to raise. And when life is good, give me a grateful heart for all your many blessings. May this day and every day be marked with forgiveness, compassion, generosity and joy and, above all, the peace which passes understanding. Make my day into your day, dear Lord, and all for your love's sake. Amen.

Cathy Roskam

Quien Soy Yo   Who Am I

Quien soy yo? ... Who am I?
Aun no se ... I still don't know.
I sit and wonder what will be ... que sera, que sera,
quien sere? Quien sere? ... Who am I? ... Who am I?
I hope to grow and be ... who knows?
Crecer, crecer y ser ... no se?
Espero ser algo incredible
incredible I hope I'll be.
Y realizar bastantes cosas
and accomplish many things
to see the world and all it's treasures
tesoros quiero ver de el mundo
espero hacer, I hope to be
I hope to be, espero hacer
for now I know not who I am
no se quien soy por el momento
pero con tiempo lo sabre, but in due time this I will know.
Quien soy yo? Who am I?
Soy mi futuro ... I am my future.

Thea Westerult

Untitled

Father, I ask You to bless my friends, relatives and those that I care deeply for, who are reading this right now. Show them a new revelation of Your love and power. Holy Spirit, I ask You to minister to their spirit at this very moment. Where there is pain, give them Your peace and mercy. Where there is self-doubt, release a renewed confidence through Your grace. Where there is self-doubt, release a renewed confidence through Your grace. Where there is need, I ask you to fulfill their needs. Bless their homes, families, finances, their goings and their comings. In Jesus' precious name. Amen.

Crucial

Untitled

Face-to-face,
beneath a golden tent of sky,
limbs snaked together
floating on cloud pillows
in the morning mist,
I have...
I have forgotten my name.
I only remember yours,
chanted like a prayer under my breath.

I inhale. You exhale.
One heart beats
in the sweetness of the stillness of this timeless omnipresence,
suspended high above the restless world.

Upon our return,
wrapped in a luminous cloak of memory,
trailed by the fragrance of
yellow rose incense
and the music of the spheres,
the very earth softens beneath our feet.

Nia Woodbine

I Feel

I'm lost in my own misery
I don't know which way to go,
or which path to choose, I'm bound
to win, but I feel I'm bound to lose.
Why do I feel this way, who knows?
But I do know every time I close my eyez
my brain glows, it tells me 2 move, but I
always stand still, because man I feel,
crome stone man steel. "Boy to Man," the years
have flew, his growth has grew, and his mind
is constantly searching for "new." He choses
to drive in the "wrong" direction. He choses
to rise out of physical aggression. I will
show passion. I will show love, not hate.
Positive can "chill" but negativity is looking for
"bait." I won't provide that bait, I provided enough.
I was standing with the title of positive actions.
Now I'm at the bluff of a flower.
I feel I've lost power, within myself, and
within my friends, Lord can it ever lose, because
I won't let it win.
I chose not to sin.
It must be terminated.
It is no longer a friend.
I'm desperate to change ways,
like the world changes days.
As I awake, I steer from eyez
that look from the skies, as
it begins to daze

people look at my picture
and read the phrase,
"so I've chosen
some bad ways."
But closed my palms and I prayed.

Donay Davis

Is He Able

Is He able to heal this pain?
Is He ready to explain these terrible
things we call death, yes, death.
Because I need to know. Because
I have strong beliefs.
But I feel so weak
I can not sleep I can not eat
trying to understand rest in peace so...

Is He able to understand me?
Is He able to know that I can feel that someone?
Is He able to know that I can miss that someone?
Is He able to know that I can love that someone?
And most of all, is He able to heal me?

Here I stand before You
trying to understand why did You
take my friend why did you let it end?
He meant the world to me and many others
it was one thing he taught me, how to
glorify Your name, halleluiah. And for that I
thank him because I haven't changed my ways.
And in Jesus' name I pray so.

Is He able to understand me?
Is He able to know that I can feel that someone?
Is He able to know that I can miss that someone?
Is He able to know that I can love that someone?

Is he able? Yes.
Is he able? Yes.
Is he able? Yes.
Is he able? Yes. To heal this pain.

Rayniel Del Valle

Untitled

The rain is like God, and the Roses are people.
God helps the people live and grow strong.
But remember, sometimes you have to help God too.

Leigh Singer

PART 4:

We Are Powerful
Beyond Measure

Shine On

We shine on we shine on
We shine on we shine on
We shine on we shine on
We shine on we shine on

A star shining in the dark
With out the dark I wouldn't shine as bright,
Blessed the divine creations that we be
I know my imagination is the only limitation
On my creations
Turning Negativity into Positivity
Caterpillar into butterfly so we can fly and be free

We shine on we shine on
We shine on we shine on
We shine on we shine on

D. Cross

My Mother's Arms

My Mother's arms have caressed me tightly
since the tender age of two
when she clung frightfully to that raggedy ole bear
as the trees clawed at her windows,
on those windy, sleepless nights.

They held me tighter still when she was then
and danced on mama's shoe tops
to Duke's swing, Papo's mambo, and Marvin's soul.
His grip began to loosen
in the summer that she turned 16
when that boy that knew that girl that knew her said:
"We should get to know each other"
as their knowledge of each other grew,
so too did the space between her inter-locking fingers,
slowly slipping silently into the murky dark of tomorrows
    to come.
At 20, her vice-grip returned, as my eyes glimpsed her beauty
    for the very first time.
She has known and loved me always, since before
    I knew myself
you see, my mother's arms have caressed me tightly since
    the age of two.

anonymous

Confession Prayer for Lent

Lord this is my cry for direction. There is so much we have to
    talk about.
There is so much I have to thank you for.
Your love is so strong.
I want to thank you for everything you have done in my life
You bless me everyday
I know I am not the person you want me to be
I still do things that are inspired only by worldly desires
But deep in my heart I wanna live and do right
There's so much I want to change inside, but I need your help
You have brought me a long way ...but I know I have a long
    way to go
Show me want you want me to do
We're hurting down here Lord.
Keep us wrapped in your arms
Lead us away from danger
...and for those who don't know you, show them your love
Keep us protected father
I'll see you when I get home.
AMEN

Incarcerated Youth, USA

Prayer for Everything

Father God, I thank You for my mother, my father and all of
my family and friends.

I ask You to protect all of them with all Your might as I ask
You to protect me.

Let there be love and light around the world. Love us all.

I send my love and well wishes to everything that exists.
And I ask You, Dear Lord, to provide guidance to those who
are lost.

And I ask You to forgive me for my sins.

God let there be love and protections for the animals and the
plants too.
God I pray to You my wishes so humbly.
Because it is what I hope for in my heart, I ask You to
heal us all.

Only You know why things happen,
so I put my trust in you Lord.

Renoly Santiago

Untitled

As I crisscross through the corridors of my complacency
I am overcome by the cries of 1,000,000 emcees.
Like ME, they too have seen the armageddon of our block,
and hurriedly scampers towards their concrete meadows,
in search of their forgotten flock
although it is said that "time waits for no man",
it seems that the big hand has tripped the little hand,
just so we could catch up.
SO AWAKEN!
All my slumbering brothas and sistas
LET NOT
this call-to-arms go unanswered
LET NOT
the repercussions of our regret
enslave us once again
like our oppressors of yester-year.

anonymous

A Woman Unfolding

A woman unfolding like a bird with
closed wings but only I have
opened mine to fly surviving the growing
pains and even the responsibility I have
gained the wind call me to fly then I
look and see that this woman
unfolding has turned into a lovely
black butterfly with a mind strong
like one of the world leaders I have
become the essence of my ancestors and the
heart of the nation who smile upon me to be
all that I can be because as the
world can see I am unfolding
like no other man woman or child.

Tiffany Collins

You Can Light a Candle

My mother died from AIDS.
When she passed away
my friend told me
you can light a candle
and pray for her
and it will help you a lot.

So
I bought a candle for my mother
I put picture by it
and I prayed for her.

It helped me
cause
when you light a candle,
even if you don't pray to that person
you can talk to that person.
Even though that person can't talk back to you
you'll feel better
cause of a lot of things
you let off your chest.

anonymous

Question, Contemplate, and Then Create

Question, contemplate, and then create
Know you don't know
And do you believe in fate?

My thoughts crowd my brain, and drive me insane
So I gotta speak my mind
I'm just tryin to stop time.

I hope you're filled with anticipation
Cause my one goal in life is to infect this great nation
I love this country with all my heart
But I can't help thinkin' we've been wrong from the start
It's clear to me that we're all spoiled
Simply by our reliance on foreign oil.

Question, contemplate, and then create
Know you don't know
And do you believe in fate?

Bad men tell lies, causing mothers to cry
Their evilness is obvious
Got that look in their eyes
Their skin's stretched thin over metallic frames
Blood runs dry inside collapsed veins
They feed on fear and what it contains
Joints squeak as they try and place the blame
Need to be oiled so they take aim
At innocent lives and other's domains.

Their greed is infinite
Like the stars in the sky
Wish a comet would fall
And they would all die.

And I'll be there with Bob Dylan
Me and him just sittin 'n chillin
As they're hung by their necks
For all their crimes and their sinnin

But who am I kiddin?
I know this won't help with all the pain they've inflicted
It's just like I predicted
Their terror consumes, from coast to coast
Desperately looking for new hosts
Their lies spread out like branches on a tree
Cause they know the truth will set us free.

Question, contemplate, and then create
Know you don't know
And do you believe in fate?

Free, like Socrates on trial for his life
Not giving in to this so-called democracy
Do you see things how they really are?
Tangled in illusion and possibility
Trying to figure out this hierarchy.

Got to understand it's all in your head
Just thoughts represented in a physical form
Separate and alone, we are torn

Like an apple from its tree
It's how things must be
Like an apple from a tree
It's how things must be.

Question, contemplate, and then create
Know you don't know
And do you believe in fate?

Joey Schaefer Schoenbohm

Untitled

Let us be together.
Let us eat together.
Let us be vital and radiate truth together.
We shall not denounce anyone and never entertain negitivity.

Traditonal Thai Buddhist Mealtime blessing

Translated by the children at Love Children's Club International,
Chiang Mai, Thailand
(www.lcic-thai.com)

I Am a Seeker

I am a seeker
A seeker of mystical experience

A seeker of

dreams

I seek to escape

the prisons of my mind

The prisons I create

The prisons that create me

I find solace in the vibrancy

of a tulip

The wind in the rainbow

The rivers in the sky

The

wave of a butterfly's wings

I smell the

Amazon

In me

The wake of

eternity

I am a seeker

A seeker of dreams.

Jason Robards III

Dear Most High

Dear Most High,

We pray for the spirits of our children to be healthy and whole, to be healed from degradation; to be healed from greed, to be healed form anxiety and pressure; to be healed from the desire to live in a false society; We pray for the youth and innocence of our children to cling to them like the mist of a cleansing rain. We pray for truth and honesty and peace to be their guiding mantra. We pray that they nurture Gaia, (mother earth) and in doing so preserve the spirits of their future generations. We pray that our ancestors will never abandon the children. Each night they will give them dreams and the shoulders to stand tall. We pray for our children to inherit a world that lives the true meaning of peace, and Bliss is an everyday reality. We pray for our children to know a world where there are no weapons, where words can only heal and a song is continually in their hearts.

Dear Allah, God, Oludamare, Buddah,

I thank you

Debra Adero Ferguso

PART 5:

Your Voice

THE GATHERING

THE GATHERING

Afterword

This collection of words is so powerfully charged with the thoughts, reflections, and dreams of everyone involved.

I am humbled.

I have chosen to summarize this effort and its importance with the words of Archbishop Desmond Tutu. His niece was baptized at St. Mark's and was the first baby in the Los Tres Reyes celebration. My dear friend Lloyd Casson is his close associate and first quoted these words to me.

Archbishop Tutu describes something of what *The Gathering* attempts to achieve, to be, with the South African term *ubuntu*. He says

> It speaks of the very essence of being human. When we want to give high praise to someone we say, "Yu u nobuntu;" "He, so-and-so has ubuntu." The you are generous, you are hospitable, you are friendly and caring and compassionate. You share what you have.
>
> It is to say, "My humanity is caught up, is inextricably bound up, in yours...We say, "A person is a person through other persons." It is not "I think therefore I am." It says rather: "I am human because I belong, I participate, I share." A person with *ubuntu* is open and available to others, affirming of others, does not feel threatened that others are able to do good, for he or she has a proper

self-assurance that comes from knowing that he or she belongs in a greater whole and is diminished when others are humiliated or diminished, when others are tortured or oppressed, or treated as if they were less than who they are.[1]

[1] *No Future Without Forgiveness*, Doubleday, New York, 1999, p. 31.

Acknowledgments

Thanks to God for the opportunity to live, love, be healthy, and be creative. Thanks to anyone who has every extended themselves with a kind word, thought or deed to me.

Thanks to Tim Holder for suggesting that I work with Lucas.

Thanks to Lucas Smith for his loving heart and razor sharp mind.

Thanks to Larry Marshall for his loving support. Thanks to Cathy Roskam and Nell Gibson for their faith in me. Thanks to my spiritual family,my mother Adreinne, my father Amos, the Houstons, the Otis's, the Martin's. Especially Amos, my brother, the late Brenda Otis, my sister, Brenda Otis my sister-in-law,mother Cora, John, Dawn and her family,Soma, Brandon, Syndney Marie ...a ray of hope, Tony Martin, Marion Elaine, Thaddeus Bruce, Theddia, Aunt Corienne, Avis, David, Katie and Steven Burgan and Steve's family, Minnie Fryer, Burt Gibson, Erica, Kathy Chase, James Solomon Benn, Anne Duquesnay,Julio Herrera, Dave Burnett, Rob and Delores Schoenbohn, Eileen Turzo, Steve Mercer.

Lloyd Casson, Carl Maultsby, Ana Hernandez, Clay Morris, Julia, Sandra, Sam, Lois Bohevesky, Edward Winslow, Stephanie Marshall, Keith Middleton, Gabriella Neri, Stanley and Larry Banks, Sam Jacobs, the late Webster Lewis, Stanton Davis, the late Charlie Maljar, Celeste, Phil Rosen and his family, Terry Monaghan, the late Noel Pointer, Kevin, Frank Koopman, producer, Byork Lee, director, Arturo Vera, Dr. Owen Jander of Wellesley College, the late Danny Scarbourough, Steve Johnson, Vishnu Wood and Peggy Cole, Bob Brustein of the American Repertory Theatre at Harvard for remembering me his book. Thanks to Maggie Edson and Dr. Westerhoff for their insightful support of my work at Kanuga. Beloved Kanuga. Thanks to the ECVA. Thanks to Jay Robards the third, my guardian angel and longtime friend through it all. Thanks to Eve Ensler and James Lescene. Also to Paul Chandler, the late Kenny Hale and Mother Hale, the inspiration from their words will always stay with me. George Brown of Kool and the Gang, my longtime friend of the spirit, the late Grover Washington and his wife Christine, John Blake, violinist, Dr. Gibbs, Sid Simmons and his late wife Syndney, the late David Vella of Austrailia, who started SOMEWHERE OVER THE RAINBOW, Mark Styles, Peter Angell, Ted Reinhert, Jack Waddell, Shirley Austin of the Shirelles, Jay Hoggard, Onaje Allen Gumbs. I want to thank my brothers in KOOL and the GANG for Ronald, Robert, DT, and the late Claytus Smith, and George for giving me the first positive example of building spiritual community in an artistic setting. Thanks to Kathy and Donald Boyce, voice of the boogie. Donald you were my voice of hope in the darkest of times. Thanks to all my arts-in education friends. Special thanks to Charlene Cambridge, Michelle Bernard, Dianne Duggan, Kristen Murphy, Larry Rolla and Dawn Crandell, for their help with this project. Thank also to Kathy Schrier, Jane Ives, Howard Katzoff, Susan Fenley, Diana Feldman, Saul Ruben, Jocelyn, Ben Jacobs, Diane Matyas, Veronica at COAHSI, Lorna, Laura Jean, Christine and Joanne at COAHSI, Sadja Mussawir of the Temple of the Arts in Staten Island, Juanita , Becky Garrison, Dr. Scopes at P754X. The staff at P754X, The staff at P751M, the Staff at the YMCA of Staten Island, The Jiving Lindy Hoppers of London. Jerry Sieck, The Marymount College Arts-in Education Staff especially Bob, Steve and Mary Kay, The Single Parent Resource Center Staff, Lisa Marie, The CAT Team Jim, Lynda Z. Akanke/ Rhonda McLean Nur, Debra Kennedy Baker of PS 399 in Brooklyn. Elizabeth Swados, John McGiness, Joe Giacolone, Nancy Myers, Helen Lau, Ellen Harris, Maria Ayala, Angela and Rafael at the United Way, Yako, and Baruch Israel. Thanks to the gang at Trinity Lutheran Renee Davis, Pastor Micheal, Gretchen and the late Jesse Anthony...all the students in the entire school I love you all, Delores Cooper, Debra Eisenhaut, the staff at COAHSI, Estina, Carol Maillard and Joy Hooks, Ron, Thomas and Joe of CES.

Thanks to Renee Felice, La, Saundra Miller, Lauria Trapp, Nanette Domingos, Ron Clearfield and his wife, Celine, and the late Salli Billinghurst, ACTV, Annie Shaver Crandell and the late Keith Crandell, Dr Fu Zhang, Dr Woo, the late Stephanie Pukit, Carol, Bridget and Nancy. Thanks to the St. Mark's family, the Diocese and the National Church for your support. Jerry Long, Frank Morales, Marlena and Micheal, John DeNaro, Caleia Soumana, Clark Trafton and Louis, Pat Thompson, Marti and George Diaz, Kendra McIntosh, Father Julio Torres, the vestry of St. Mark's. Especially Cynthia and her family, Georgina, John and Josh, Annette Hendrickse, Claire McPherson and his wife, Gina, Kathy Volpe. Ed..... we miss you. The late Peggy Stewart, the late David Urban, Danspace , the Poetry Project and the Ontological Theatre. Bill Russell, Lola, Steve Facey, Claudia. The St. Mark's Free Choir: Jill, Elizabeth Stiles, Elizabeth Allison, Fred Alston, Anthony, Earl Gianquinto, Rob, Linda Tarnay, Benji Dunn, Kathy Chase, Rob Schoenbohn, Tyrone Aiken.

All my sisters and brothers in the spirit that I have worked with in the Episcopal Church on so many wonderful services.

The E Mass 'crew' Kevin Delaney and Veronica, Lawrence Singer and Leigh, the EMass Band ,

D CROSS , the Missionary Men, the Remnant, Crystal, Kurtis Blow ..the E Mass Band.

Thanks again to the Church Publishing staff, especially Frank, Lucas and Diane.

THAT'S IT. Jeannine/ Jahneen......smile